EDITOR:

Jack Harrison
jharrison@mortons.co.uk

PAGE DESIGN:

Craig Lamb
design_lamb@btinternet.com

COVER DESIGN:

Holly Furness

PRODUCTION EDITOR:

Pauline Hawkins

REPROGRAPHICS:

Paul Fincham
Jonathan Schofield

ADVERTISING:

Billy Manning
bmanning@mortons.co.uk

MARKETING MANAGER:

Charlotte Park

COMMERCIAL DIRECTOR:

Nigel Hole

PUBLISHING DIRECTOR:

Dan Savage

PUBLISHER:

Steve O'Hara

PRINTED BY:

William Gibbons and Sons,
Wolverhampton

IBSN:

978-1-911276-39-5

PUBLISHED BY:

Mortons Media Group Ltd
Media Centre, Morton Way,
Horncastle, Lincolnshire, LN9 6JR

Contents

ACKNOWLEDGEMENTS:

Selecting and narrating 300-or-so images of a woman deemed to be the most photographed in the world has been no simple task, and there are plenty of people to whom I owe my thanks for their work on this project.

Designer Craig Lamb has done a superb job of flowing the chosen photography throughout the publication, and I am indebted to production editor Pauline Hawkins for assistance in honing and polishing my words to fit this commemorative 132-page edition.

The incredible wealth of content in the Press Association archive must also be mentioned, as should the work of Paul Fincham and Jonathan Schofield, who have ensured that each selected image is completely ready for printing.

Given the choice available, settling on a cover image and design was perhaps the most challenging part of the production process, so my gratitude goes to designer Holly Furness for her work (and considerable patience!).

Finally, I must also highlight the support of those closest to me during the work undertaken for this volume, and for other publications I work on.

Compiling and editing this picture-led journey through the life of Diana, Princess of Wales has been fascinating and at times emotional. I suspect, and certainly hope, that those who read the following pages will find it as enjoyable and poignant as I have.

Jack Harrison, editor

Diana, Princess of Wales

1961-1997

"Diana was the very essence of compassion, of duty, of style, of beauty. All over the world she was a symbol of selfless humanity. All over the world, a standard bearer for the rights of the truly downtrodden, a very British girl who transcended nationality. Someone with a natural nobility who was classless and who proved that she needed no royal title to continue to generate her particular brand of magic."

Earl Spencer
Diana's brother
September 6, 1997
Westminster Abbey

The People's Princess

Lady Diana Spencer grew up as a shy young girl in the quiet English countryside, yet in her 36 years she found a way into the hearts of millions of people from across the globe. As a graceful princess, a devoted mother and a champion of various worthy causes she became and remains one of the most adored and recognised public figures of modern times.

In the days following her untimely and tragic death following a car accident in 1997, millions across Britain and throughout the world found varying ways to pay their respects. A week later, thousands poured into London to line the streets as her coffin made its way to and from an emotionally charged funeral.

It was between these two unforgettable and historic events that British Prime Minister Tony Blair described Diana as the People's Princess – perfectly symbolising her unique place in history.

This is her story...

The young Diana alongside her brother Charles, Viscount Althorp, in the late 1960s.

From the Spencer family photo album, Diana is pictured with the Shetland pony Soufflé at her mother's home in Scotland during the summer of 1974.

Her early years

The People's Princess was born as the fourth child of John, Viscount Althorp and Frances Spencer on July 1, 1961, at their family home of Park House near Norfolk's Sandringham estate.

Diana became the couple's third daughter after Sarah and Jane, but sadly they had suffered unimaginable heartbreak just a year prior to the new arrival when their first son John died shortly after his birth. Desperate for a male heir, the Viscount had been particularly affected by events and the newborn girl was a week old before a name was chosen. On August 30, she was christened at St Mary Magdalene Church near the family's abode.

The Spencers' desire for a baby boy continued, and with Diana approaching her third birthday they announced the birth of Charles, who arrived on May 20, 1964. While it seemed as if the perfect family was complete, the strain of losing a child and being so obsessed with having a son and heir had begun to tell on the marriage.

Diana's parents separated in 1967, and she initially lived with her mother in London. During the early part of 1968, however, Lord Althorp won custody of the children and subsequently moved them to their ancestral seat in Northamptonshire after he succeeded to his father's title and became Earl Spencer in 1975.

Despite the emotional turmoil, Diana's was a privileged upbringing and the Spencer family had enjoyed a close relationship with the British monarchy for a number of generations. Both Earl Spencer's and Lady Althorp's mothers had served as ladies-in-waiting to the Queen Mother, and Earl Spencer himself had been a royal equerry for both King George VI and a young Queen Elizabeth II.

And the ties didn't end there; the Queen was among the guests at the Spencers' Westminster Abbey wedding in 1954, a highlight of the social calendar that year; Diana's first home at Park House was leased from Her Majesty; and because the royals often spent holidays at the neighbouring Sandringham House, Diana was close to the Queen's younger children, Prince Andrew and Prince Edward.

Education for Diana began under the supervision of her governess, Gertrude Allen, before she attended a private school in Gayton and then a girls-only boarding school near Diss – both in Norfolk. In 1973 she joined her sisters in Kent at the West Heath Girls' School where she excelled at sport, music and dance; although she struggled academically and actually failed her O levels twice. Her community spirit, something with which she'd become synonymous in later life, also shone through and she received an award for her work.

After one term at a finishing school in Switzerland, Diana returned to London and moved into her mother's apartment with two school friends. Belying her upper-class roots and education, she pursued a relatively simple life and was determined to earn a portion of her living as she took a series of low-paid jobs as a dance instructor, party hostess and nanny, among others.

Settled in London, Diana's mother bought her a flat in Earls Court as an 18th birthday present, as her daughter started another new job as a nursery teacher's assistant at the Young England Kindergarten in Pimlico. Described by her family and friends as shy and unassuming, this comparatively peaceful existence seemed to suit Diana, but it was not to last.

A year later, in the summer of 1980, a friendship with Charles, Prince of Wales – heir to the throne of Great Britain – began to blossom into a romance. Rumours swirled about the relationship and the world's media set their focus on the 19-year-old love interest of the world's most eligible bachelor.

A three-year-old Diana at Park House in Sandringham.

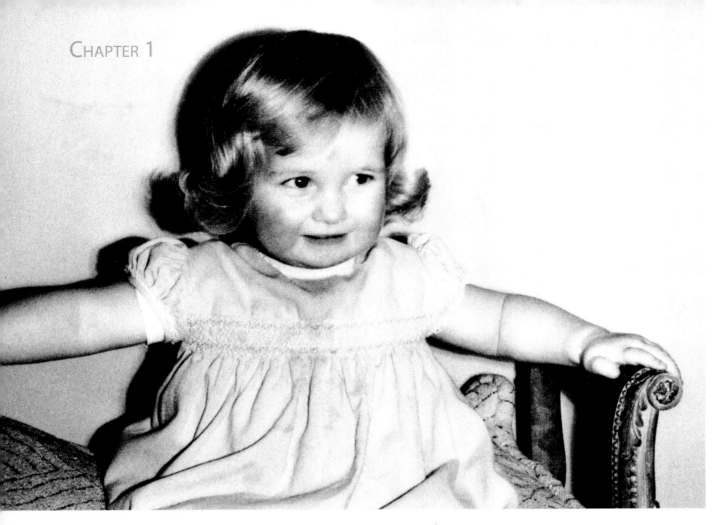

Diana enjoys a stroll in her pram around the grounds of the Sandringham estate during the summer of 1963.

Shortly after her second birthday, Diana is pictured inside her home at Park House.

A picture of Diana as a toddler, taken at her home during 1965.

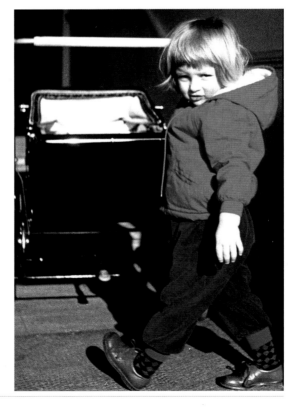

Diana plays with her younger brother Charles, Viscount Althorp, in the August heat of 1967 within their family residence in Norfolk.

A game of croquet was among the activities enjoyed by Diana during a holiday to Itchenor, Sussex, in 1970. The small village was home to Peter Shand Kydd, who married Diana's mother in 1969 and became the future princess's stepfather.

Lady Jane Spencer stands outside the Guards Chapel at St James Park in London on April 20, 1978, with her new husband Robert Fellowes. They are joined by Jane's younger sister and bridesmaid Diana, along with other members of the wedding party.

Once she had been linked romantically to Charles, Prince of Wales, the British press was eager to share a glimpse into the life of the woman who might be a future queen of Great Britain. During their courtship, Diana was pictured several times while working at a kindergarten in London's St George's Square.

Press photographers followed Diana day and night as speculation mounted that she and Charles, Prince of Wales, were romantically involved. Here she is seen smiling having stalled her new car – a Mini Metro – in front of the cameras as she left her apartment for work on the morning of November 17, 1980.

Charles and Diana

The romantic life of Charles, Prince of Wales, had become a public and press obsession by the start of the 1980s, and the world waited impatiently to find out when and with whom the future king – now in his 30s – would settle down.

He was certainly not short of suitors, having had a number of relationships (and several more rumoured dalliances) with various acquaintances, one of whom was Lady Sarah Spencer – Diana's eldest sister. It was during this time, in the latter part of 1977, that Charles and Diana first met.

A romance was not initially on the cards, but the pair remained friends. Three years later in the summer of 1980, they were both guests at the same country weekend – Diana watching Charles play polo – and it was at this point that the prospect of a more serious union became apparent. They soon grew closer, especially in the wake of the compassion and support Diana offered following the murder of Lord Mountbatten, the Queen's cousin and Charles's mentor, at the hands of the IRA.

The prince invited 19-year-old Diana on a sailing weekend to Cowes aboard the Royal Yacht *Britannia*, and it was not long before he took her to Balmoral Castle in Scotland to meet the Royal Family. Queen Elizabeth II, the Duke of Edinburgh and the Queen Mother all approved of Charles's new sweetheart.

Despite the age difference, and apparent lack of similar interests, the new couple seemed clearly smitten and continued courting in London throughout the remainder of 1980 and early into the next year.

After six months of dating, the Prince of Wales proposed marriage to Lady Diana during a private dinner at Buckingham Palace ahead of her planned trip to Australia. Charles had intended for Diana to use the three-week break to consider his proposal, but she accepted immediately.

By this time, public, press and media furore surrounding the couple was at fever pitch. Still living in her London apartment and working at the nursery, Diana in particular was the subject of much attention – the world eager to find out more about this 'ordinary' girl who had captured the heart of the monarch-to-be. Somehow the couple managed to keep their engagement secret until Diana returned from Australia, at which time Buckingham Palace issued a statement saying: "It is with the greatest pleasure that the Queen and Duke of Edinburgh announce the betrothal of their beloved son the Prince of Wales to Lady Diana Spencer."

With the engagement official on February 24, Diana left her job (she was actually the first royal bride to have a paying job before her engagement) and moved to Clarence House for a short time, and then Buckingham Palace. Set to become an official member of the Royal Family, she also began making public appearances with her new fiancé, her first being a glamorous charity ball in March 1981 where she was introduced to actress Grace Kelly, the Princess of Monaco. And while Diana tried to adapt to this new life in the spotlight, the royal household brought together the grand plans for what was being dubbed 'the wedding of the century' set to take place on July 29 at St Paul's Cathedral.

The Prince of Wales
and his fiancée
Lady Diana enjoy
a walk during their
holiday to Balmoral
in May 1981.

The day it seemed like everyone was waiting for had finally arrived as Britain's future king Charles, Prince of Wales, and Lady Diana Spencer officially announced their engagement to the world at Buckingham Palace on February 24, 1981. Hunger for news about the new royal couple was unprecedented, and of particular interest was the ring chosen by Charles's bride-to-be. Diana selected a large engagement ring that featured 14 solitaire diamonds surrounding a 12-carat oval blue Ceylon sapphire set in 18-carat white gold, made by Crown jewellers Garrard.

Lady Diana is pictured in the Knightsbridge area of London in November 1980. While the 19-year-old was dating Charles by this time, their relationship was not public knowledge – although the UK press had certainly got wind of the burgeoning romance and were reporting as such.

Just a little more than a month since their engagement, Charles and Diana pose with Queen Elizabeth II at Buckingham Palace on March 27, 1981. The photograph was taken shortly after a meeting of the Privy Council – a formal group of advisors to the British monarch.

Charles kisses Diana goodbye as he prepares to leave for a five-day tour of New Zealand, Australia and Venezuela on March 29, 1981.

Just a matter of days before their wedding, Diana and Charles embark on a visit to the Cheshire Regiment – part of the historic Prince of Wales' division – at Tidworth on July 24, 1981.

A casually clad Charles rests on a fence with Diana during a stroll in the Scottish countryside in May 1981. The pair had been relaxing on holiday at the royal residence of Balmoral as they approached their wedding day, which was set for late July.

Diana wowed in a black taffeta evening gown as she appeared at her first official royal engagement on March 9, 1981, seen here talking to Princess Grace of Monaco. The event took place at London's Goldsmiths' Hall in aid of the Royal Opera House Development Appeal.

The royal party greet crowds from the balcony of Buckingham Palace following the Trooping the Colour ceremony in June 1981. From left to right are Lady Diana Spencer, the Prince of Wales, Lord Nicholas Windsor, the Duke of Edinburgh, Queen Elizabeth II, Angus Ogilvy, the Duchess of Kent, Alexander Earl of Ulster, Prince Andrew and the Duke of Kent.

On July 27, Charles and Diana are seen leaving St Paul's Cathedral after their wedding rehearsal. Following just behind are Prince Andrew and Prince Edward.

The wedding

Britons young and old wake from a night in sleeping bags on the morning of Tuesday, July 28. Some of these people had arrived two days before the wedding to secure a vantage point outside St Paul's Cathedral.

The build-up

Despite the relatively short engagement, the excitement and anticipation that built for the wedding of Charles and Diana was on a scale never before seen for such an event. Wednesday, July 29, was the chosen date, and it was designated as a public holiday in Great Britain which would allow thousands to descend on London and millions more to watch at home...

Every aspect of the royal event gained press attention, and the choice of wedding ring was among one of the most hotly discussed topics in the run-up. Collingwood of Conduit Street in London's opulent Mayfair was chosen as the jewellers – and the same nugget of Welsh gold used to make the wedding rings of the Queen Mother in 1923, the Queen in 1947, Princess Margaret in 1960 and Princess Anne in 1973 was selected.

Mrs Vi Lee, landlady of the Prince and Princess of Wales pub in London, made the most of the publicity to incorporate Charles and Diana into her swinging sign.

Royal wedding souvenirs were produced and purchased in huge numbers throughout the summer of 1981. Prestigious British company Wedgwood was among those to create unique items, such as this vase displaying the portraits of the bride and bridegroom.

In scenes mirrored across the country, Arthur Dibley of Walworth in London busily decorates his house with flags, shields and pictures of the future Prince and Princess of Wales.

British soldiers take a break from mountaineering exercises in the Italian Alps on July 23, and pay tribute to the royal couple with a special message written into the snow.

From the moment the engagement was announced, public excitement just continued to grow and grow. The fairy-tale wedding and the fairy-tale princess were the subjects of constant coverage, and Lady Diana was greeted with adoration at her public appearances. One such example was her first visit to Royal Ascot in June 1981.

CHAPTER 3

The UK's Royal Air Force aerobatic team, the Red Arrows, performs a special Prince of Wales Feathers formation over Caernarfon Castle to mark the royal wedding. The historic venue in north-west Wales was the location of Charles's investiture in 1969.

London's Hyde Park was the scene of celebrations on the eve of the wedding, this stunning firework show rounding off proceedings.

If it could be related to the royal wedding it was. This London Routemaster bus was painted with ribbons and bows to look like a giant wedding present.

The big day had finally arrived, and Charles gives a final wave to the crowds before entering St Paul's Cathedral with his brother Prince Andrew.

The wedding party

◆

Never before, and perhaps not since, had there been a wedding like this one – and it was reflected in the number of notable figures and dignitaries who attended from around the world. The guest list was a who's who of British and European nobility, politicians and diplomats, and of course the closest friends and family of the bride and groom...

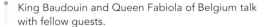

The Queen Mother and Prince Edward make their way through the gathered crowds to St Paul's.

King Baudouin and Queen Fabiola of Belgium talk with fellow guests.

US first lady Nancy Reagan arrives at Fitzroy Square in London on July 28. Mrs Reagan was to attend the wedding as the official representative of America. Her husband, President Ronald Reagan, enjoyed a strong relationship with the UK but had unfortunately been unable to make the event.

Members of the Royal Family – including the Queen, Princess Margaret, the Duke of Edinburgh and Prince Andrew – on the steps of St Paul's with Earl Spencer following the wedding service.

Princess Grace of Monaco, who Diana had met during her first official royal engagement, joins the congregation.

Princess Alexandra – the Queen's cousin – and her husband Angus Ogilvy arrive for the ceremony.

The Duke of Edinburgh joins Diana's mother, Frances Shand Kydd, in the procession back to Buckingham Palace following the wedding service.

Eagerly awaiting the arrival of the bride and bridegroom are the Queen, the Duke of Edinburgh and the Queen Mother.

Sarah Armstrong-Jones, 17, and Catherine Cameron, six, wave to crowds en route to St Paul's. The girls were two of five bridesmaids to Diana along with 13-year-old India Hicks, 11-year-old Sarah-Jane Gaselee and five-year-old Clementine Hambro.

Waving to the royal couple as they head back to Buckingham Palace are the Duke of Edinburgh, Princess Anne, Frances Shand Kydd, Captain Mark Phillips, the Queen, Earl Spencer, Prince Andrew and the Lord Mayor of London Colonel Sir Ronald Gardner-Thorpe.

The mother of the groom and father of the bride head towards Buckingham Palace for the wedding breakfast.

The wedding party poses for the official group photo, with the new Prince and Princess of Wales at the centre.

They say it's the bride's prerogative to be late, but Lady Diana arrived at St Paul's with her father almost perfectly on time for the scheduled 11.20am ceremony. Her dress, valued at £9000, was made of ivory silk taffeta decorated with lace, hand embroidery, sequins and some 10,000 pearls. Designed by Elizabeth and David Emanuel, it featured a 25ft-long detachable train. The veil was ivory silk tulle spangled with thousands of tiny hand-embroidered mother-of-pearl sequins – held in place by the Spencer family diamond tiara. Two of Diana's bridesmaids, India Hicks and Sarah Armstrong-Jones, are following behind.

The ceremony

◆

The wedding itself was full of all the pomp and pageantry that had been in evidence during the build-up, and was led by the Archbishop of Canterbury, Robert Runcie. Charles and Diana had selected St Paul's over the more traditional Westminster Abbey because of its increased capacity: they needed it, with a congregation of 3500 in place to witness them become the Prince and Princess of Wales...

Charles and Diana acknowledge the Queen and Duke of Edinburgh as part of their traditional Church of England wedding service.

Surely one of the proudest moments for any father – Earl Spencer escorts his daughter down the aisle.

Nerves were clearly present for both the bride and bridegroom during the momentous occasion. As they read their vows, Diana accidentally changed the order of Charles's name calling him 'Philip Charles Arthur George' rather than 'Charles Philip'. He also made an error, saying that he would offer her 'thy goods' instead of 'my worldly goods'. Diana did not promise to 'obey' her fiancé after the word was removed at the couple's request, something that caused a press and public sensation at the time.

The Prince and Princess of Wales make their way back down the aisle at St Paul's to the sounds of Edward Elgar's Pomp and Circumstance No. 4. Three choirs, three orchestras and a fanfare ensemble played during the service, with other music and songs including the Prince of Denmark's March, I Vow to Thee, My Country and Britain's national anthem God Save the Queen.

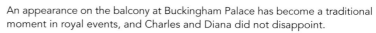

An appearance on the balcony at Buckingham Palace has become a traditional moment in royal events, and Charles and Diana did not disappoint.

The bride and bridegroom join together at the altar, as Archbishop of Canterbury Robert Runcie begins proceedings.

Charles and Diana emerge on the steps of St Paul's and greet the public as a married couple for the first time.

In perhaps the day's most iconic and memorable photo, the royal couple delight the crowds by sealing their marriage with a kiss.

Balloons join the escort of the Blues & Royals – a regiment of the Household Cavalry – as they accompany Charles and Diana from Buckingham Palace to Waterloo Station.

The honeymoon

Following the ceremony, Charles and Diana made their way back to Buckingham Palace. Later that day they were driven across London to Waterloo station – Princes Andrew and Edward attaching a 'just married' sign to their vehicle. They then embarked the British Royal Train to start their honeymoon…

The couple wave to waiting crowds as they emerge from Romsey Station in Hampshire.

The Prince and Princess of Wales are driven through Romsey as they head for Broadlands. They spent three days at the English country house before flying to Gibraltar to begin a cruise of the Mediterranean.

Departing Waterloo, the newlyweds wave from the British Royal Train.

At RAF Andover near Southampton, Diana waves goodbye before she and Charles take off for Gibraltar.

Diana is greeted on arrival at the quay in Gibraltar – thousands gathered behind her to catch a glimpse of the new princess.

Clearly in a merry mood, Charles and Diana depart aboard the Royal Yacht *Britannia* for their Mediterranean cruise.

Having returned from their honeymoon at sea, the royal couple enjoyed a holiday at Balmoral Castle along with the Queen and other members of the Royal Family. Here, the Prince and Princess of Wales enjoy a stroll along the banks of the River Dee.

Charles and Diana stop for press pictures during their break in Scotland, August 1981.

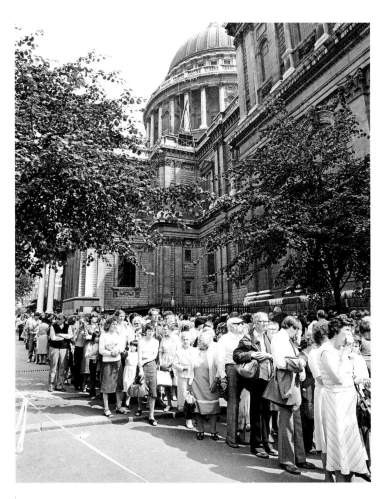

A huge queue on The Mall in London doubles back on itself the Saturday following the wedding. The crowds are waiting to get into St James's Palace where the royal couple's gifts have gone on display.

Thousands stand patiently to enter St Paul's two days after the royal wedding. The venue is still decorated as it was for the ceremony, and the signed register of marriages is also on display.

Diana chats with oil rig workers during her tour of the Charlie platform at Forties – the largest oilfield in the North Sea – on September 4, 1985.

Her Royal Highness the Princess of Wales

In the blink of an eye and a whirlwind of romance, the quiet and shy Lady Diana Spencer had become the wife of Britain's future king. The narrative was one of a fairy-tale that culminated with the lavish ceremony at St Paul's Cathedral, but as the euphoria of the royal wedding faded Diana had to tackle the various challenges her new life would present.

Her official title became Her Royal Highness the Princess of Wales, and her role demanded appearances at a succession of public events and functions. It felt as if she was on a near-constant merry-go-round of organised visits during which she would greet the general public – often gathered in their thousands to catch a glimpse of or even meet her.

Given that Diana had never craved the spotlight, the young princess coped admirably and took to her royal duties with charm and elegance that soon won favour with the press and people alike. The Royal Family was by no means unpopular at this time, but Diana had managed to evoke something more.

She was just being herself – and that's what set her apart. Diana was at ease when meeting the children, nurses and patients she encountered during her various royal engagements to nurseries, schools and hospitals, and they responded by singling her out for affection. There was a feeling that she enjoyed spending time with 'normal' people, perhaps owing to the fact her own life would never be normal again.

Yet she appeared just as relaxed in grander settings, whether it was political formalities, significant meetings or international tours. The height of the hysteria came at one such formal event when she took to the dance floor with actor John Travolta following a White House gala dinner in November 1985.

Even more remarkable is that Diana had navigated this intense period of her life while also starting a family. The arrival of William in 1982, and Henry in 1984, was met with great excitement, and the obvious love and devotion that Diana afforded her children only increased the adoration she received.

Charles and Diana visited New Zealand during April 1983, and here the Princess of Wales appears in formal wear during an official engagement.

Queen Elizabeth II, the Duke of Edinburgh, and the Prince and Princess of Wales stand for photos with the leaders of the 10 European Economic Council nations who had enjoyed a lunch at Buckingham Palace on November 26, 1981. The group, including British Prime Minister Margaret Thatcher – second from the right – were visiting the UK for a two-day meeting of the council at Lancaster House.

Diana's fashion was always a hot topic. This tartan outfit by Caroline Charles was certainly well received while the princess attended Scotland's Braemar Games in September 1981.

On October 27, 1981 – the first of a three-day visit to Wales – Charles and Diana greet crowds at Caernarfon Castle.

In the same Glass Coach used for her wedding, the Princess of Wales makes her way to Westminster on November 1, 1981, for the State Opening of Parliament – her first appearance at the institutional British political event.

The Princess of Wales meets Chelsea Pensioners in June 1983. This engagement took place at the Royal Hospital Chelsea – a retirement and nursing home for British Army veterans in London.

Diana arrives at Bristol's Royal Hospital for Sick Children in February 1983.

On one of many visits to education facilities, Diana is surrounded by youngsters at a pre-school play group in Gloucestershire during November 1982.

Charles and Diana are pictured on November 25, 1982, at a ceremony in the Welsh town of Barmouth to officially name a new lifeboat – *The Princess of Wales*.

It wasn't just in Britain that Diana was capturing the hearts of the public. She's pictured here in April 1983 adopting the hongi – a traditional Maori greeting where participants press their noses together.

A worker at the Keiller sweet factory in Dundee, Scotland, welcomes the Princess of Wales during her visit in September 1983.

Charles and Diana exit a banquet in Novia Scotia, Canada, along with Canadian prime minister Pierre Trudeau – left. As the couple departed the dinner on the evening of June 16, 1983, the Prince of Wales was heard to comment to the press pool of his wife: "Isn't she lovely?"

Donning the Spencer family tiara, as worn at the royal wedding, Diana joins Charles at the State Opening of Parliament at the House of Lords in November 1984.

Charles and Diana embrace during a break in the Prince's polo match at Cirencester Polo Club in July 1985.

The royal couple visited Italy in April 1985, and as part of the trip went to the Vatican where they met Pope John Paul II.

Joined by its organiser Bob Geldof, Charles and Diana prepare to take their seats for Live Aid on July 13, 1985. The star-studded music concert at London's Wembley Stadium raised millions of pounds for famine relief in Africa and, along with the royal wedding, became one of the memorable events of the 1980s.

For many people, when they think of the Princess of Wales, there is one enduring image they conjure. As part of a royal visit to the United States of America, Charles and Diana stayed at the White House on the night of November 11, 1985, where they attended a gala dinner hosted by President Ronald Reagan and his wife Nancy. Also present was actor and star of musical-drama Saturday Night Fever John Travolta, who has since recalled that another guest had told him that Diana would be delighted to dance with him. At around midnight, Travolta duly invited her out on to the floor. The rest is history.

British Prime Minister Margaret Thatcher and her husband Denis hosted a dinner in honour of the Royal Family at Downing Street on November 20, 1989. The Prince and Princess of Wales were in attendance, along with Russian cellist Mstislav Rostropovich, his wife Galina Vishnevskaya and their daughter Elena.

In a Rising Sun dress, Diana was suitably attired for her and Charles's visit to Japan in 1986.

Visiting the 13th/18th Royal Hussars' training exercise on Salisbury Plain during the summer of 1988, Diana is kitted out in army-issue khaki overalls.

Diana presents the FA Cup trophy to Wimbledon captain Dave Beasant following his side's unexpected triumph over the mighty Liverpool at Wembley on May 14, 1988.

Diana presents dancer Natalia Makarova with an Evening Standard Theatre Award for Best Performance of 1985. The honour was given to Makarova by the Princess of Wales on the night of July 17, 1986, following the dancer's appearance in a gala performance of Onegin – the ballet for which she won the award – at London Coliseum.

Vanderbilt Racquet Club members the Princess of Wales, Lord Willoughby De Broke, left, and Charles Swallow, right, are joined by German tennis ace Steffi Graf in March 1988.

Diana is joined on the balcony of Buckingham Palace on June 15, 1991, by the Duchess of York and the duchess's daughter Beatrice. The trio is looking up at an RAF flypast following the Trooping the Colour ceremony.

Well-wishers present the Princess of Wales with numerous bouquets on May 8, 1989, as she embarks on a royal engagement to Delta Tennis Centre in Swindon.

The Prince and Princess of Wales pose for photographers during their skiing holiday with Charles's brother Prince Andrew, the Duke of York and Andrew's wife Sarah, Duchess of York. Diana and Sarah became close during their respective marriages to the royal brothers, with the quartet and their children regularly spending time together such as this 1987 break in the Swiss resort of Klosters.

At a national tennis tournament in Nottingham during July 1991, Diana shares a joke with British three-time grand slam champion Virginia Wade, second left, and singer Cliff Richard.

During her September 1991 visit to Pakistan, Diana is pictured with the Khyber Rifles near the historic Khyber Pass.

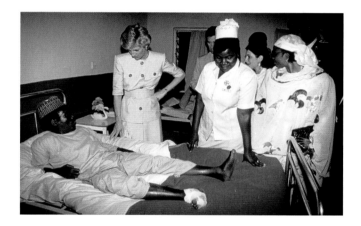

A rain-soaked Charles and Diana meet with Italian tenor Luciano Pavarotti after his concert at London's Hyde Park on July 31, 1991.

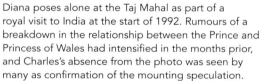

The Prince and Princess of Wales go on a royal walkabout during the second day of their visit to Czechoslovakia in May 1991.

Diana poses alone at the Taj Mahal as part of a royal visit to India at the start of 1992. Rumours of a breakdown in the relationship between the Prince and Princess of Wales had intensified in the months prior, and Charles's absence from the photo was seen by many as confirmation of the mounting speculation.

As part of a visit to Africa in March 1990, Diana meets a patient at a Cameroonian hospital.

Charles and Diana introduce baby William to press photographers as part of a specially arranged event at their Kensington Palace home on December 22, 1982 – the young prince having just turned six months old.

A future king arrives

The big question going into the 1980s was: "When will the Prince of Wales marry?" Following the wedding, that was quickly replaced by the next hot topic – the tantalising prospect of a royal baby.

Growing up as one of four siblings, Diana had always yearned for a large family and less than six months into their marriage – on November 5, 1981 – it was officially revealed that she and Charles were expecting their first child the following summer.

On June 21, 1982, came the day the nation had been waiting for as Diana gave birth to a son in the private Lindo Wing of St Mary's Hospital in London; the newborn becoming second in line to the British throne behind his father.

A week later, Buckingham Palace officially announced that he would be named William Arthur Philip Louis – and he was christened as such at the royal residence on August 4.

Diana and William – the youngster approaching his seventh birthday – prepare for a cycling trip in Tresco during a 1989 summer holiday to the Scilly Isles.

The public get their first glimpse of their new prince and future king, as Charles and Diana emerge with William from St Mary's the day after his arrival.

William is the focus of attention from Queen Elizabeth II, Charles, Diana, the Duke of Edinburgh and the Queen Mother on the day of his christening.

William enjoys the sunshine with Charles and Diana in Auckland, New Zealand. The young prince, not yet a year old, accompanied his parents on their official visit to the country in April 1983.

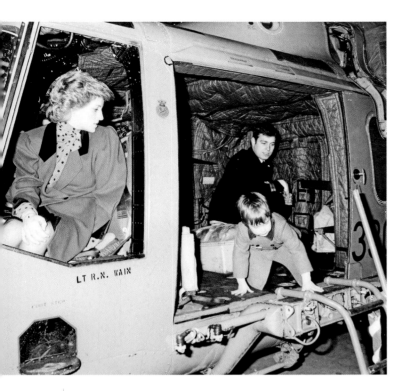

Under the watchful eye of Diana and his uncle Prince Andrew, William explores a military helicopter on board HMS *Brazen* during a visit to the Royal Navy frigate on February 6, 1986.

Ahead of his second birthday, William enjoys a kick-around with his father in the gardens of Kensington Palace on June 12, 1984.

At Smith's Lawn in Windsor on May 17, 1987, a four-year-old William sits on Diana's lap as the pair watch the Prince of Wales playing polo.

The new group of royal youngsters look at home on the balcony of Buckingham Palace, appearing as part of the Trooping the Colour ceremony to mark Her Majesty's official birthday on June 16, 1984. Princess Anne's daughter Zara Phillips talks to Prince William, with Lord Frederick Windsor – son of Princess Michael of Kent – and Princess Anne's son Peter Phillips completing the quartet.

Two-year-old William excitedly rushes into St Mary's Hospital on September 16, 1984. He was there to visit his mother and new baby brother, who'd been born the day before.

Charles and Diana prepare to say goodbye to William as he arrives for his first day at kindergarten on September 23, 1985.

Charles and Diana held a photocall at Kensington Palace on December 14, 1983, to mark William turning 18 months old the following week.

Diana and William make the most of some rest time during a holiday to Mallorca in August 1987.

As members of the Royal Family gather for a photo at the christening of the newest royal arrival on December 21, 1984, it's William who steals the show.

Charles and Diana introduce Prince Harry to the world as they leave St Mary's Hospital on September 16, the day after his arrival.

The royal family grows

Excitement surrounding the arrival of Prince William had only just begun to subside when the Prince and Princess of Wales welcomed a second child, and second son, on September 15, 1984.

He was christened by the Archbishop of Canterbury at Windsor Castle three months later on December 21 as Henry Charles Albert David, but he would soon become known as Harry – a name that stuck.

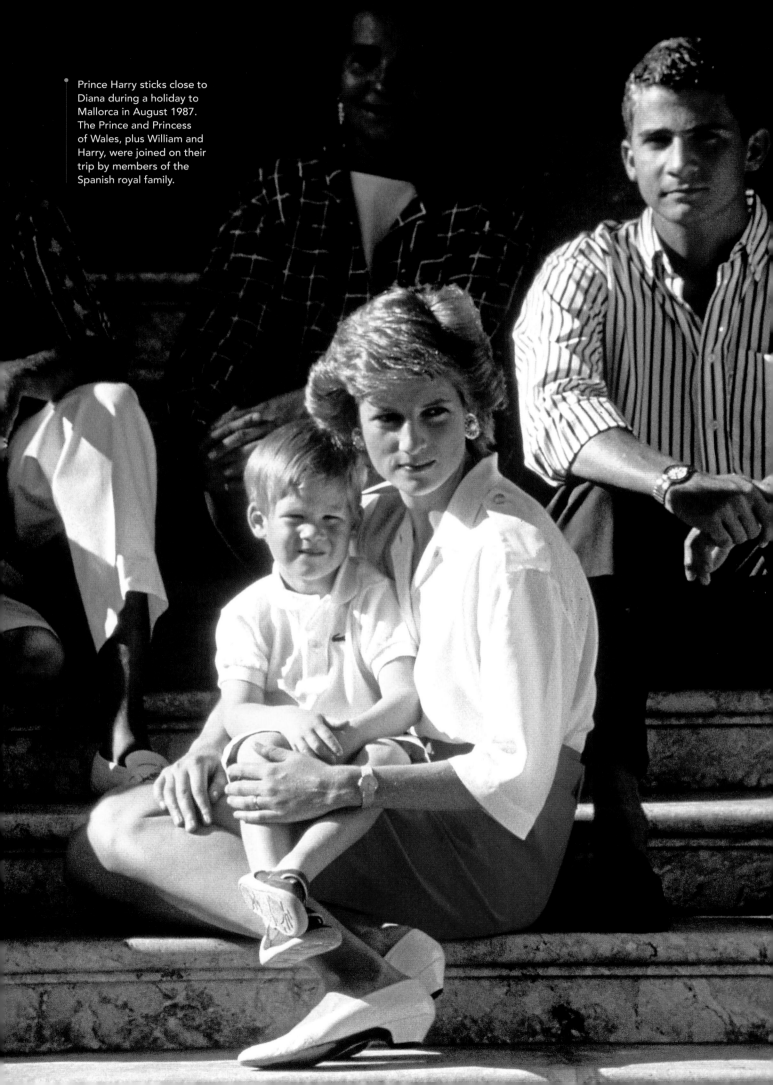

Prince Harry sticks close to Diana during a holiday to Mallorca in August 1987. The Prince and Princess of Wales, plus William and Harry, were joined on their trip by members of the Spanish royal family.

The Prince and Princess of Wales pose with Harry following his christening at St George's Chapel in Windsor.

Diana carries Harry on to the Royal Yacht *Britannia* on August 7, 1985, as the Royal Family prepares for a break in the Western Isles.

The Princess of Wales watches as Harry tries out the cockpit of a Harrier GR5 during a visit to RAF Wittering on May 28, 1991.

Harry showed early signs of his playful character with this signature 'royal salute'. He and Diana were pictured leaving Portland Hospital in central London having just visited the Duke and Duchess of York and their newborn daughter Princess Beatrice on August 10, 1988.

Having turned three years old just 24 hours earlier, Harry arrives for his first day at nursery school in West London on September 16 – with a Thomas the Tank Engine bag in hand.

Watching rugby would go on to become one of Harry's favourite pastimes, and here he's seen enjoying the action at a Wales versus Australia match at Cardiff Arms Park with Diana in October 1991.

Harry, the Queen Mother and Diana leave Buckingham Palace on June 16, 1991. The trio are en route to the Trooping the Colour ceremony in London.

Prince Harry arrives with his mother at the Royal Albert Hall on February 20, 1991. They are set to attend the Mountbatten Festival of Music charity concert, performed by the massed bands of the British Royal Marines.

Charles and Diana show their delight aboard the Royal Yacht *Britannia* on May 5, 1985, having been reunited with William and Harry following a 17-day separation for an official tour of Italy.

Prince Harry waves to photographers as he gets ready for his first day at nursery school on September 16, 1987. Doting brother William had joined Charles and Diana to see him off.

Two princes

As the sons of Charles and Diana, William and Harry were subjected to similar levels of press attention as their parents – the spotlight shining especially bright on William as the elder of the brothers and the most likely to one day ascend to the throne.

While royal life had its incredible privileges, growing up in such an environment was certainly a unique experience and presented challenges to even the most simple of day-to-day tasks. Diana, however, was adamant that the pair would have the opportunity to enjoy a much wider range of activities than would be usual for a royal child.

During their formative years she organised her own childcare rather than relying on a royal nanny, she selected their schools and planned their outings – and whenever her schedule allowed she accompanied the princes when they left the confines of their home at Kensington Palace.

Given the nature of their upbringing, William and Harry spent a lot of time with fellow Royal Family children, becoming close to their cousins Peter and Zara Phillips and both Princess Beatrice and Princess Eugenie. They also developed a deep brotherly bond themselves, one that remains evident to this day.

William shields his eyes from the sun as he sits on the steps of Marivent Palace in Mallorca where he, Harry, Charles and Diana are on holiday. Joining them are King Juan Carlos of Spain in the centre and Queen Sofia seated next to Charles. Also present for the photograph taken on August 13, 1988, are the Spanish royal couple's children Christina, Elena and Felipe.

The Prince and Princess of Wales relax with William and Harry during their June 1989 holiday to the Scilly Isles.

Five-year-old Harry arrives excitedly for his first day at the Wetherby School in London's Notting Hill on September 15, 1989. Elder brother William, seven, is already a pupil and the two are welcomed by headmistress Frederika Blair-Turner.

William, Diana, Harry and Charles arrive in Bath for the wedding of a family friend in May 1989.

The Princess of Wales rides a chair lift with William and Harry on April 10, 1991, during a skiing trip to Lech in Austria.

The Princess of Wales during her interview with Martin Bashir for the BBC's Panorama current affairs series. Broadcast on November 20, 1995, it has featured among lists of the most-watched programmes in British TV history.

Andrew Morton's controversial biography of Diana was released in May 1992, and was the first major public insight into the saga that eventually resulted in her and Charles's divorce.

The Queen of Hearts

The 1980s began with a fairy-tale romance, but by the time the 1990s dawned the marriage of the Prince and Princess of Wales had irrevocably broken down – a turn of events that was about to be sensationalised by the world's media.

Newspapers, at first maintaining the perceived happy marriage, suppressed any inkling of problems between the royal couple – this despite the fact the relationship had started to crumble as early as 1985. Their separate lives had become public knowledge by 1987, at which time the press had begun to report on the troubles almost daily. Charles and Diana kept up appearances for the remainder of the decade and into the start of the next, but by 1992 the problems between them had reached the point of no return.

In February of that year came the now-famous photo of Diana sitting alone in front of the Taj Mahal during her and Charles's visit to India. It wasn't especially unusual for public figures to pose solo in front of the iconic monument – Charles himself had done so 12 years earlier; the princess however cut a lonely and isolated figure, and the image became the first public evidence that while the formal union was still in effect the relationship was in fact at an end.

It took just a few further months for the full details to emerge, many of them being aired with the publication of *Diana: Her True Story* – a book by royal biographer Andrew Morton. The pages gave an unprecedented insight into the royal marriage and Diana's life, the most shocking revelations being Charles's affair with former girlfriend Camilla Parker-Bowles and the princess's own extra-marital relationship with Major James Hewitt. The book also told of Diana's battle with bulimia and thoughts of suicide.

Later in the year the royal couple embarked on a state visit to South Korea where it was painfully apparent that they had grown distant. In news met with little surprise, Prime Minister John Major announced to the British Parliament in December that they were to formally separate.

The period that followed, through until their divorce became official on August 28, 1996, saw the British Royal Family at its lowest ebb of modern times – the scandal of Charles's affair reflecting badly on the institution. The separation and divorce of Prince Andrew and the Duchess of York, and Princess Anne and Captain Mark Phillips did not help matters.

Charles sought to improve his and the monarchy's public image in a televised interview with broadcaster Jonathan Dimbleby in June 1994, during which he confirmed the stories about the rekindling of his romance with Mrs Parker-Bowles while he was still with Diana. While the PR exercise went some way to countering the criticism, the goodwill Diana had built – combined with her own adept ability to project a favourable public persona – meant she retained her immense popularity. For many in the public, and particularly in the press, it was a case of taking sides.

In response to the Prince of Wales, Diana appeared on BBC's Panorama programme in November 1995 for a remarkably open discussion with journalist Martin Bashir. Millions across the UK tuned in to hear the princess describe her post-natal depression, intimate details of the breakdown between her and Charles, her tense relationship with other members of the Royal Family and a stunning claim that her estranged husband didn't really want to become king.

Diana also revealed that she didn't expect to ever become queen, but on the subject of her own future expressed a desire to become what she described as a "queen in people's hearts". In the months before and after the divorce was confirmed she set about defining exactly what her new role would entail as Diana, Princess of Wales.

As she entered into a new chapter, Diana embarked on various foreign trips championing a number of causes close to her heart. Here she's pictured in Lahore, Pakistan on May 23, 1997.

Diana meets children at a
royal event in May 1992.

While the details of her strained relationship were making the pages of the national newspapers on a near-daily basis, Diana had a formal role as Princess of Wales to continue. Part of that was attending such events as the annual Trooping the Colour ceremony – this one taking place on June 13, 1992. Joining Diana on the Buckingham Palace balcony are the Queen, Prince Charles, the Queen Mother and Lady Gabriella Windsor, daughter of Prince Michael of Kent.

The Prince and Princess of Wales are pictured at the national cemetery in the South Korean capital of Seoul during an official visit to the country in November 1992. The obvious tension between the couple led many to suggest that the widely reported problems between them were irreconcilable.

Diana in London in March 1993 – this was among her first public appearances in the wake of her separation from the Prince of Wales.

Trainee electrician Danny Walters kisses Diana's hand as she greets crowds during a walkabout on March 10, 1993. Her visit to Southwark in South London was to open the Riverside Hostel for single homeless women.

Diana chats with a group of hard-hatted construction workers at Oxford Brookes University and AIDS centre on May 26, 1993.

Diana suffers from an attack of the giggles at the Wimbledon tennis tournament on July 4, 1993. She was in attendance with her mother Frances Shand Kydd to watch the Men's Singles final between Americans Pete Sampras and Jim Courier.

This service at Southsea Common was among many held to mark the 50th anniversary of D-Day in June 1994. The Princess of Wales speaks to a veteran of the critical Second World War engagement during a walkabout after the commemorative event.

While there were certainly moments of friction between Charles and Diana during their separation, as both parents and officials of the monarchy they remained amicable enough to support their children and fulfil their roles. Here they are pictured at Liverpool Cathedral on May 30, 1993, following the Battle of the Atlantic commemorative service.

Diana attends a charity dinner in Versailles, France, on November 28, 1994. The event was held in aid of Barnardo's and La Fondation pour l'Enfance.

Having arrived by helicopter, Diana and her lady-in-waiting Anne Beckwith-Smith walk with Lord Richard Attenborough towards the new Attenborough Arts Centre in Leicester on May 27, 1997. The Princess of Wales had opened the new facility earlier that day.

The Princess of Wales remained a popular figure not just in Britain but across the Commonwealth, and here she's seen shaking hands with well-wishers outside the Sydney Conference Centre in November 1996 during the second day of a visit to Australia.

In her capacity as honorary Air Commodore of the base, Diana watches as a Harrier Jump Jet is prepared for take-off at RAF Wittering on September 28, 1995.

There was great debate among officials and the press alike as to Diana's future role once she and Charles were separated and then eventually divorced. The princess clearly had an idea of the type of public figure she wished to be, and she continued with various engagements such as this one on December 6, 1995, when she opened the English National Ballet School in London.

On the occasion of her 36th birthday on July 1, 1997, the Princess of Wales leaves the Tate Gallery's Centenary Gala Dinner carrying gifts received from friends.

Diana speaks to ballerinas from the English National Ballet on June 3, 1997, after they gave a gala performance of Swan Lake at the Royal Albert Hall.

While Diana might have felt that the press attention she received would lessen in the wake of her separation and subsequent divorce from the Prince of Wales, it was in fact the opposite. The media was obsessed with her, conveying her every move, and in the summer of 1997 the coverage went into overdrive as speculation mounted that she was romantically involved with Egyptian businessman Dodi Fayed – son of former Harrods owner Mohamed Al-Fayed. On August 21, 1997, reporters and photographers followed Diana as she left her gym – the princess saying nothing in response to questions about the relationship. Soon after, she joined Dodi in the south of France having accepted his invitation to holiday with him and his family at a private compound.

US first lady Hillary Clinton – wife of President Bill Clinton – greets Diana at the White House during a visit to the American capital in June 1997.

Diana, William and Harry ride in a horse-drawn sleigh on March 27, 1994, as they leave their hotel while on holiday in Lech, Austria. The trio is joined by the princess's friends, Catherine Soames and Kate Menzies.

A mother

While Diana looked to carve out a new role as the Queen of Hearts in the wider world, her first and foremost concern was to ensure she dedicated the appropriate time and energy to what had always been her most pressing concern – being a parent to William and Harry.

As had been the case before her and Charles's separation, the Princess of Wales insisted on giving her two sons as many 'normal' life experiences as possible. They were known to have dined at McDonald's and played video games, and Diana even took them to Walt Disney World in Florida on holiday.

At the same time, she ensured they remained humble and aware of the difficulties faced by people around the world as she involved the young princes in her charity work. It's clearly an upbringing that had an effect, with the pair at the forefront of various national and international causes today.

The young princes join their mother on a boat ride at Niagara Falls during a visit to Canada in October 1991.

Diana had her differences with Charles and the Royal Family, but they were always put aside for the sake of her children. Here, she joins her sons for a photo at Windsor Castle along with Charles, the Queen and other representatives of the monarchy. The event was organised on March 9, 1997, to commemorate the confirmation of Prince William.

Diana holds the hand of Prince Harry, with Prince William just behind as they walk towards their car on August 10, 1988. The youngsters and their mother have just visited the Duchess of York and her new baby, Princess Beatrice, for the first time.

Diana, William and Harry take to the slopes at Lech, Austria, in March 1994.

Diana always wanted her children to have typical experiences for boys their age at that time. Of course, being second and third in line to the throne meant nothing was ever quite typical, and the event pictured was no ordinary trip to the cinema as the princess and her two princes met stars of Steven Spielberg's Hook at the Odeon in London's Leicester Square. Left to right in the line-up are Phil Collins, Bob Hoskins, Robin Williams and Dustin Hoffman, who all attended the film's premiere on April 7, 1992.

On April 13, 1992, William and Harry got to enjoy the new £2.4 million dinosaur exhibit at London's Natural History Museum. Diana accompanied her young sons for the tour.

Diana and her two boys enjoy a water ride as part of a day out at Thorpe Park in April 1993.

The Princess of Wales and Prince William arrive for the traditional Christmas Day church service on the Sandringham estate in 1994.

The Princess of Wales and Prince Harry inspect an honour guard as part of a visit to the barracks of the Light Dragoons in Germany on July 29, 1993.

RIGHT: Prince Harry clearly enjoys his time on the Splash Mountain ride at Disney's Magic Kingdom in Florida in August 1993. Diana, however, seems less keen as she hides on the back row. **BELOW:** During the same trip, Diana watches the Indiana Jones stunt spectacular alongside Harry Soames, the son of her close friend Catherine.

The Duchess of Kent joins Diana and William in the Royal Box at Wimbledon on July 2, 1994. Action on court was the Women's Singles final between Spaniard Conchita Martínez and American Martina Navratilova.

Scottish racing driver and Formula One star David Coulthard gives Diana and Harry a behind-the-scenes tour of the Williams team garage on July 10, 1994.

William and Harry are joined by their mother on May 7, 1995, for the Heads of State Service for VE Remembrance Day. The event was held in London's Hyde Park.

Proud mother and father look on as Prince William, also joined by his younger brother, signs in on his first day at Eton College on September 16, 1995.

Diana meets children with cystic fibrosis during a visit to the Royal Brompton Hospital on April 14, 1997.

A champion

Community and giving had been important to Diana from an early age, and she backed a number of organisations in her official capacity as Her Royal Highness the Princess of Wales. Yet it wasn't a role confined just to committee rooms – she made several lengthy visits each week to the Royal Brompton Hospital where she helped comfort patients who were seriously or terminally ill.

The way in which Diana tackled the important issues also made people sit up and take notice – and she was, very shrewdly, able to maximise the exposure for the causes closest to her heart.

She became one of the first major public figures, and certainly the first royal, to broach the subject of AIDS at a time when uncertainty and misinformation about the condition was prevalent. In 1991, she met with residents of an AIDS hospice in Canada and was pictured without gloves shaking the hand of a patient – a simple act that was responsible for removing many unwarranted prejudices.

It wasn't the first time she had made such a statement either; in 1989 she was praised for publicly shaking hands with people affected by leprosy, dispelling myths about the disease.

Such kindness and compassion shown to people in need only deepened the affection the public felt for her, and charitable pursuits remained one of her major passions after the breakdown of her marriage.

However, in her new role she'd have to find different ways to go about tackling the problems of the world. The day after her divorce she announced her resignation from more than 100 positions to focus her time and resources on a smaller selection of groups and causes – AIDS, landmines, cancer, mental health and homelessness being the most notable.

Support of charitable causes began early in the royal life of the Princess of Wales. She's pictured here on January 23, 1982, with Charles visiting the Dick Sheppard School in London to back a fundraising campaign.

On a trip to Nemazuva School in Zimbabwe on July 12, 1993, Diana sits with children being helped by a charity meal scheme.

The Princess of Wales receives a gift of a sweatshirt from Wayne Taylor on October 25, 1991. Taylor was a resident at the Casey House AIDS hospice in Toronto, Canada, and was the sufferer with whom Diana first shook hands. She was quoted as saying: "HIV does not make people dangerous to know. You can shake their hands and give them a hug. Heaven knows they need it."

Diana and 10-year-old Laurence Chambers, who has cerebral palsy, go for a walk during the princess's visit on October 31, 1995, to open the National Institute of Conductive Education in Birmingham.

Diana shakes hands with William Drake, a patient at West London's Lighthouse AIDS Centre, on July 20, 1992.

At the Minapur
Old Age
Welfare Centre
in Hyderabad,
India, in February
1992, Diana
bends down to
shake hands with
an 'Untouchable'
– the lowest rung
of the country's
caste system.

Among the causes Diana chose to pursue was the eradication of landmines, and to do so she became a benefactor of the non-governmental entity known as HALO – the Hazardous Areas Life-Support Organisation. On January 15, 1997, the princess visited an active minefield in Angola, a country that has been ravaged by more than 30 years of civil war and which was still littered with millions of landmines. Having declared her support earlier in the trip for a Red Cross campaign to ban the use of mines worldwide, the princess spent time with HALO workers to learn about the demining process and even detonated a mine herself, famously uttering the words: "One down, 17 million to go" as she pressed the button.

PERIGO MINAS!

DANGER   MINES

ABOVE: Sister Lynne Frederick speaks with Diana as the princess pays a visit to Mother Teresa's home in Calcutta on February 15, 1992. Well-known nun and missionary Teresa was the founder of an organisation that provided homes for people dying of AIDS, leprosy and other diseases. While they lived entirely different existences, their desire to help the poor and needy meant she and Diana found much common ground and became acquaintances. **BELOW:** Teresa had been unable to attend when the princess was in Calcutta, but the two met briefly on February 19 at a convent in Rome.

Diana stands for a photograph in Hong Kong on April 23, 1995. She's joined by drug addicts who are undergoing treatment at a rehab centre.

Shadow Home Secretary Jack Straw, right, and new chief executive Victor Adebowale join Diana at the annual meeting of homeless charity Centrepoint on December 7, 1995.

The Princess of Wales talks to paediatric nurses learning medical skills on rubber baby models at the Tushinskaya Children's Hospital in Moscow, Russia. Diana was a patron of the hospital's trust, and visited the facility on May 16, 1995, as part of a two-day visit to the Russian capital, and later went on to tour the Kremlin and a charity that made and distributed wheelchairs.

Diana sits with two young patients on her knees during an April 1996 visit to Imran Khan's cancer hospital in Lahore, Pakistan.

Outside Sydney's Royal Rehabilitation Centre, the Princess of Wales stands with patient Ben Robertson and his family on November 3, 1996.

Young patient Lydia Hewer looks at a Valentine's Day card with Diana during the princess's visit to London's Great Ormond Street Hospital in February 1997.

As part of a visit to highlight Cystic Fibrosis Week on April 15, 1997, Diana learns about the daily medication regime of patient Nicky Welsh at the Royal Brompton Hospital.

Diana addresses the gathered media at the American Red Cross HQ in Washington, DC, on June 17, 1997. The princess spoke on the issue of landmines, ahead of a dinner later that evening in the US capital to raise much-needed funds in support of those tackling the problem worldwide.

Residents of Chicago give Diana a warm welcome as she goes on a walkabout at Northwestern University on September 4, 1996. The princess was in the US city on a charity fundraising mission.

On a January 1997 trip to observe the work of the British Red Cross in Angola, Diana enjoys a cuddle with one of the many babies at the Kikolo health post.

Staff and youngsters chat with Diana at Centrepoint's Cold Weather Project in London's King's Cross on March 10, 1997. The facility provides food, beds and respite for 47 young homeless people.

Diana watches medical staff at work in an Angolan hospital in January 1997.

Diana is pictured at Luanda airport in Angola on January 16, 1997, following her visit to the country on behalf of the Red Cross.

An icon

At 19 years old Diana was thrust into the spotlight, an unwitting and unwilling by-product of a nation's desire to see its future king, after numerous false starts, finally find true love. She had become the girl others wanted to be, the shining star everyone wanted to see and the glamorous princess everyone wanted to meet. For better or worse, it was a level of fame she maintained for the rest of her life.

Her every style statement – and occasional fashion faux pas – was followed, pored over, dissected and copied as soon as she burst on to the world stage as Charles's bride-to-be, and women worldwide tried desperately to replicate her inimitable style in the years that ensued. In the eyes of the people she was the perfect princess, and so she became the perfect wife, then the perfect mother.

Whether it was the British tabloids, international newspapers or global magazines, the press wanted to tell her story and feature her on their cover. Her free spirit and unmistakable charm certainly made for many a memorable moment, both when she was with the Prince of Wales and in her life after.

Diana broke the mould for how a member of the Royal Family should behave, and gave the institution a much-needed injection of modernism with her willingness to indulge in and interact with popular culture rather than be removed from it. She never seemed totally at ease with the attention lavished upon her, but it cannot be denied that she embraced her celebrity status. She was certainly able to use it to enhance her own image when needed, and give exposure to the various causes with which she was associated.

Behind that intelligent promotion, however, what truly endeared Diana to the people who followed her was that she stayed true to her roots. For all the experiences she had, in a life that few of us can imagine living, she somehow continued to be 'one of our own'.

Even when images appeared of her at a high-powered global function or glitzy ceremony attended by the world's richest and most powerful, there remained a perception that she was still just that quiet, shy and humble young princess who had captured so many hearts all those years before.

It was this remarkable feat that maintained her connection with the British people, and with those from countries all over the world. She did it in a way that no one had before, and perhaps no one has since.

On September 8, 1995, there was a special charity screening of new Hollywood hit film Apollo 13 at the head office of United International Pictures in Hammersmith, London. In attendance along with the princess was, left to right, Rita Wilson (wife of Tom Hanks), one of the film's stars Tom Hanks, director Ron Howard, producer Brian Grazer and his partner Gigi Levangie.

At a charity fundraising gala dinner in Chicago in June 1996, Diana dances with local businessman Michael Wilkie.

The Princess of Wales enjoys the action on Centre Court at Wimbledon in July 1994.

Actor Anthony Andrews accompanies Diana at the royal gala premiere of his new film Haunted on October 27, 1995. The screening was held in aid of the British Red Cross 125th Birthday Appeal and the European Anorexia Trust – two organisations supported by the princess.

ABOVE: At a charity dinner in Paris on September 25, 1995, Diana meets American magician David Copperfield. **RIGHT:** Earlier, the princess arrived for the event with French politician and first lady Bernadette Chirac. Among the organisations being supported was Great Ormond Street Hospital, of which Diana was the president.

Diana addresses members of the council of fashion designers of America at New York's Lincoln Centre on January 30, 1995.

While Diana had a sometimes tempestuous relationship with journalists, by and large she was open to interacting with the mainstream press – certainly to a much greater degree than any member of the Royal Family had ever been in the past. Whether it was in a bid to better connect with the people, ensure her side of the story was heard or promote her charity endeavours, she always seemed relaxed in interviews and comfortable with answering questions on a range of topics. She's pictured here with PA News' royal correspondent Peter Archer during a chat in Angola where the princess was campaigning for the eradication of landmines.

As patron of the National AIDS Trust, Diana was in attendance at the Concert of Hope on World AIDS Day – December 1, 1994. The event, at London's Wembley Arena, featured British boy band Take That, seen here greeting the princess. Left to right are members Robbie Williams, Jason Orange, Howard Donald, Mark Owen and Gary Barlow.

Pakistan cricketer-turned-politician Imran Khan welcomed Diana to his cancer hospital in Lahore in February 1996. She's pictured during the visit with Khan, his now former wife Jemima and her mother Lady Annabel.

LEFT: During a Washington, DC, dinner held in aid of raising money for breast cancer research on September 24, 1996, Diana presents fashion designer Ralph Lauren with a humanitarian award. **ABOVE:** Earlier the same day, the princess and Washington Post owner Katherine Graham listen to a speech by US first lady Hillary Clinton.

Having accepted the United Cerebral Palsy charity's Humanitarian Award from former US secretary of state Henry Kissinger, Diana makes a speech to the 800 guests at the ceremony in New York's Hilton Hotel on December 11, 1995.

New York

TV presenter Jeremy Beadle and photographer Terry O'Neill speak with Diana at Harrods department store on October 15, 1996. The princess had just launched a new book in aid of research into heart and lung disease.

At the Empire in Leicester Square on February 12, 1997, Diana wows as she arrives for the premiere of Richard Attenborough's latest film In Love and War.

Diana poses for press pictures with Angolan foreign minister Venancio de Moura, part of her four-day visit to the country in January 1997.

The Princess of Wales meets children outside the Shri Swaminarayan Hindu Mission, in Neasden, north London, on June 6, 1997.

The Princess of Wales chats with TV and radio host Terry Wogan in April 1997.

Diana is pictured outside the Royal Geographical Society in London where she made a keynote speech at a conference on landmines. During the address, on June 12, 1997, she reiterated her backing for the anti-mines campaign and insisted it was a humanitarian cause and not a political one.

In August 1997, Diana visited the country of Bosnia where she met victims of landmines. Ahead of her flight home, she poses with some French SFOR soldiers at Sarajevo's airport.

CHAPTER 12

Tragedy in Paris

◆

August 31, 1997

As Diana, accompanied by Dodi Fayed, left the Hôtel Ritz Paris in the very early hours of Sunday, August 31, no one could have predicted or imagined the events about to unfold.

In an attempt to flee paparazzi attention, Diana and Dodi were driven out of the hotel at around 12.20am by the Ritz's deputy head of security Henri Paul. Also in the car was Trevor Rees-Jones of the Fayed family's personal protection team. Heading for an apartment in Rue Arsène Houssaye, the car made its way along the banks of the River Seine and towards the Place de l'Alma underpass.

About three minutes into the journey Henri Paul lost control of the vehicle, which swerved across the two-lane carriageway and collided head-on with a pillar supporting the roof. The car then spun and hit the wall of the underpass – the combination of both impacts causing massive damage, particularly to the front half.

Photographers that had been following the foursome were the first to reach the scene. Some attempted to help; others, incredulously, continued to take pictures despite the horrific scenes they encountered. Once emergency services had arrived, both Dodi Fayed and Henri Paul were pronounced dead at the scene.

Trevor Rees-Jones, who would be the only survivor, was still conscious but had suffered several serious injuries and lacerations to his face. It's believed that Diana was also conscious when she was first found, and by 1am she had been removed from the car ready for transport to a medical facility. At that time she went into cardiac arrest, paramedics working vigorously to get her heart beating. She arrived at Pitié-Salpêtrière Hospital at 2.06am, but despite continued attempts to save her life the injuries she'd sustained proved to be fatal. Diana passed away at 4am.

As the darkness of early morning turned into daybreak, the shocking and sobering news began to filter out into Britain and the wider world as senior figures such as Prime Minister Tony Blair appeared on TV to speak to the nation. Senior representatives of the French government, including Bernadette Chirac – wife of President Jacques Chirac – visited the hospital to pay their last respects, while the Anglican Archdeacon of France, Father Martin Draper, attended Diana's hospital room and said commendatory prayers.

Later that same day, the Prince of Wales arrived in the French capital with Diana's older sisters, Lady Sarah McCorquodale and Lady Jane Fellowes. The three of them were to escort the People's Princess back home.

1. A man prays next to the mound of flowers left by members of the public outside the gates of Buckingham Palace.
2. Diana's coffin, draped in the Royal Standard, is carried off a Royal Squadron plane by servicemen at RAF Northolt.
3. A sombre and visibly shaken Prime Minister Tony Blair addresses the British nation from his home near Newcastle.
4. A shot looking back down The Mall from Buckingham Palace shows the crowds gathered at the royal residence.
5. Crowds gather outside Kensington Palace, Diana's official residence.
6. The Union Flag flutters at half-mast over the Houses of Parliament in London.
7. A photo taken in the days after her death: the world's magazine media react to the tragic events.
8. A photograph of Diana is captured among a mass of floral tributes.
9. A young girl pays her respects to Diana with a prayer.

3 4

8 9

The Queen and Duke of Edinburgh inspect the floral tributes to Diana outside the gates of Buckingham Palace the day ahead of her funeral.

A nation mourns

The death of Diana, Princess of Wales, brought with it a profound sense of grief – the like of which had never been witnessed before in the United Kingdom. People woke on the morning of Sunday, August 31, to continual and blanket news coverage on all the major TV networks, and within hours there were huge crowds flocking to royal buildings to pay their respects with flowers, cards and other tokens of their sorrow. On Monday morning, a book of condolence was opened at St James's Palace and by the afternoon people were waiting patiently to sign it in their thousands. It's believed that at some points during the week, there were 10-hour queues. Great Britain, a steadfast country famed for its stiff upper lip, laid its emotions bare for the whole world to see – and the world followed suit.

The Royal Family, including William and Harry, had been on their summer holiday at Balmoral in Scotland when details of the tragic events occurred. Sticking to protocol that had served them well for nearly half a century, the monarchy remained silent and chose not to engage in any unexpected acts of tribute such as the lowering of a flag at Buckingham Palace. The Royal Standard only flies when the Queen is in residence, and it would never be displayed at half mast because there is always a monarch – these were age-old traditions

that could not be broken. Queen Elizabeth II, who had previously proved herself to be adept at judging and reflecting on the nation's mood, had this time got it spectacularly wrong.

There was an outcry from the people, whipped up by the print media, and as plans came together for the funeral Her Majesty became public enemy number one in the highly charged atmosphere that had enveloped the country. On Thursday, September 4, the Royal Family made preparations for their return to London – stopping briefly at the gates of Balmoral to inspect the flowers and read messages. Once back in the capital, the following day the Queen made her first live broadcast to the nation in 38 years to pay tribute to Diana and explain that her actions were not from a lack of compassion or care, but driven by a desire to protect her two young grandchildren devastated by the loss of their mother. In a further show of appreciation for her subjects' will, the Union Flag was raised at half mast over Buckingham Palace.

Perhaps a grieving people had just needed a focus that week, and criticism of the head of state became an outlet for the unprecedented shock and sadness. After the address, negative feeling toward the monarchy soon dissipated and attention turned to the funeral.

The final goodbye

In the evening, on Friday, September 5, Charles, William and Harry had visited Diana's coffin at St James's before the three were driven – through huge crowds of silent mourners – behind a hearse carrying the princess to Kensington Palace. It was from her official residence that she would depart the following morning for a funeral unlike any other. High streets across the country were deserted, public events postponed or cancelled and TV schedules cleared. The only thing anyone was interested in on Saturday, September 6, was the last journey of the People's Princess.

Shortly after 9am, the coffin left Kensington Palace on a gun carriage for a procession through London's streets. In touching and memorable scenes, it was followed on foot by Diana's brother Earl Spencer, Prince Charles, his sons William and Harry and the Duke of Edinburgh after having reached St James's; 500 representatives of charities supported by Diana joining the funeral cortege behind them. The coffin also passed Buckingham Palace where other members of the Royal Family were waiting outside. It's believed that the route to Westminster Abbey was lined by more than a million mourners.

The hour-and-10-minute service got under way at 11am, attended by notable names from the worlds of politics, philanthropy, music, film and TV – a representation of the various barriers Diana had crossed in her role as a British royal. UK viewing figures peaked at 32.1 million – one of the biggest ever in the country – and it's believed that more than two billion followed the event worldwide, making it one of the most watched in history. It was perhaps best remembered for the incredibly moving and poignant eulogy delivered by Earl Spencer, as well as singer Elton John's rendition of a specially revised version of Candle in the Wind.

After the funeral had concluded, a hearse transported Diana to Northamptonshire and Althorp House. The 77-mile journey took the princess through the North London suburbs and beyond, where thousands more people had gathered to pay their final respects. In a private burial attended by just her closest relatives and friends, the Princess of Wales was finally laid to rest on a secluded island in the heart of the grounds of her family home.

Devastated mourners form patient queues outside Diana's home at Kensington Palace, preparing to pay their respects the day after her death.

Prince Harry holds his father's hand while reading messages left by well-wishers outside the gates of Balmoral Castle.

Thousands of people made their way to London in the week after Diana's passing, many laying bouquets of flowers at the gates of numerous royal residences or places of national interest. Removal of the tributes was a lengthy operation, and estimates suggest between 10 and 15 tonnes' worth had been left throughout the capital once the funeral was over.

Arriving back in London ahead of the funeral, Charles and his sons William and Harry inspect the sea of flowers placed at Kensington Palace.

As well as flowers, many mourners lit candles for the Princess of Wales outside the gates of the royal residences or places of worship. This particular tribute in York became an enduring image of the historic week.

Following a great deal of pressure, mainly stirred up by the press, Buckingham Palace flies the Union Flag at half mast on the morning of Diana's funeral. It was a complete break from protocol by Her Majesty, and so the Union Flag has since been raised any time she is not in residence. The palace has also lowered it to half mast to mark other notable deaths or times of national mourning, such as the terrorist bombings in London on July 7, 2005.

A group of Welsh Guardsmen carry Diana's coffin into Westminster Abbey, the cortege having made a near two-hour trip through the streets of the British capital.

The Queen and the Queen Mother at Westminster Abbey for Diana's funeral.

Elton John plays his rewritten version of Candle in the Wind during the service. The singer was a close acquaintance of the princess, and it was only a month prior that she'd been seen comforting him after the funeral of their mutual friend – fashion designer Gianni Versace.

Mourners gathered in London's Hyde Park to watch Earl Spencer pay tribute to his sister at Westminster Abbey via specially erected big screens.

Spectators weep in the crowd along London's Whitehall.

Italian tenor Luciano Pavarotti shows his emotion as he views Diana's coffin.

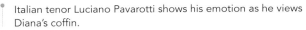

The Duke and Duchess of York arrive at Diana's funeral, along with their daughters Princess Beatrice and Princess Eugenie. The Duchess and Diana had formed a close bond during their respective years as royal brides and were known for the sense of fun they shared – the press branding them as the 'Merry Wives of Windsor'.

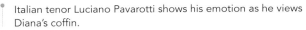

The Duke of Edinburgh, Prince William, Earl Spencer, Prince Harry and the Prince of Wales turn on to Horse Guards Parade, following the coffin of Diana during the funeral procession to Westminster Abbey. While the events that occurred behind the closed doors of Balmoral Castle in the week between Diana's death and funeral remain private, it's understood that the Duke of Edinburgh was instrumental in William and Harry choosing to walk behind their mother – reportedly advising that they might later regret it if they chose not to. To show his support, the Duke offered to join his grandsons.

Wait-times at St James's Palace were said to be as long as 10 hours as thousands visited the royal building to sign the five books of condolence dedicated to the Princess of Wales.

Frances Shand Kydd leaves Westminster Abbey after her daughter's funeral service.

The Princess of Wales's coffin is driven away from Westminster Abbey on the journey to her final resting place of Althorp House in Northamptonshire. Those who've lined the streets throw flowers in front of and on to the hearse, and a British police officer does the same as the hearse makes its way down The Mall in front of Buckingham Palace.

The Diana, Princess of Wales Memorial Fountain in London's Hyde Park.

Her legacy

Even the most ardent of her supporters would likely concede that the outpouring of emotion in the wake of Diana's death reached levels that could accurately be described as hysteria. In the weeks and months that followed, the intense atmosphere calmed into a more appropriate reflection of the princess's life and work, and those who knew her best set about establishing ways to remember her.

Various installations have been erected in Diana's memory – the most notable being the Memorial Fountain in London's Hyde Park, opened in 2004 by the Queen. Others have been built or dedicated across the UK and the world, while some – such as the Flame of Liberty above the entrance to the tunnel where the fatal crash occurred – have become unofficial tributes to the princess. While these are very visible reminders of her life, Diana's impact goes much deeper.

In the live speech Queen Elizabeth II was essentially forced into making just days after her former daughter-in-law's death, she cited how lessons should be learned from Diana's example. It's clear now that these words were far from empty. As the new millennium came into focus, the Royal Family embarked on an image makeover – a sustained PR campaign to take the institution into the 21st century. No longer would they be out of touch with the public, no more would they be seen as lacking understanding of real life – in the mould of the People's Princess they would instead connect with their subjects. Suddenly there were images of the royals meeting pop culture celebrities, visiting popular fast food chains and touring the sets of the nation's favourite TV shows. This approach would work somewhat for the older, more staid members of the monarchy, but to truly change the face of the institution they needed new blood to step forward. In William and Harry, they had the perfect young men for the job.

The princes are the embodiment of everything their mother stood for. While her efforts are certainly demonstrated by the progress made within the causes she supported, Diana's sons are quite clearly the way in which her legacy is best preserved and perpetuated. They have captured and embraced her ability to seem at ease with everyone they meet, the pair have continued their mother's work in supporting a number of charitable causes and they continue to show a steadfast dedication to their family.

As Great Britain and the wider world marks 20 years since her passing, William and Harry have ensured that the values and influence of the People's Princess remain firmly intact.

Prince William and Prince Harry speak with injured British servicemen in April 2008 at Headley Court Rehabilitation Centre near Epsom in Surrey.

William and Harry help out with Red Cross relief efforts on January 7, 2005, by packing items bound for the Maldives.

Celebrity chef Gordon Ramsay races against Prince William during the Sport Relief charity London Mile event in 2004.

The princes are pictured during a trip to the Semongkong Children's Centre in Lesotho in June 2010 where they met orphaned youngsters.

Prince Harry and the Duke and Duchess of Cambridge wave their wands on Diagon Alley – from the fictional world of Harry Potter – as part of a trip to Warner Bros Studios in Hertfordshire in April 2013.

During a visit to the Bahamas in March 2012, Prince Harry does the signature pose of Olympic sprint champion Usain Bolt – next to the athletics superstar himself.

Ten-year-old Marcela Hernandez-Rios clearly enjoys William's teaching style as he delivers an English lesson in southern Chile during December 2000. The work was done as part of his Raleigh International expedition to the country.

Prince Harry chats with pupils in a class at the Osmani school in London's Whitechapel in September 2002. The lesson, run in partnership with charity Merlin, taught pupils about the health issues faced by people in the developing world.

Residents of Mants'ase children's home in Lesotho find Prince Harry's funny faces amusing during his return visit to the facility on April 27, 2006.

Just as his mother had before, William enjoys the action during an England international rugby match in February 2002. The fixture in question was England versus Ireland in the Six Nations at Twickenham.

His mother was famed for her interaction with the public during royal walkabouts, and here William speaks with well-wishers at the official opening of the Diana, Princess of Wales Memorial Fountain in July 2004.

Just as his mother had before him, Prince William does the traditional Hongi greeting during a visit to New Zealand in July 2005.

David Beckham, perhaps the world's most famous footballer during the 2000s, enjoys spending time with Prince William on June 19, 2010, during an FA reception in South Africa.

ABOVE: William and Harry on stage at Wembley stadium ahead of the Concert for Diana – a musical event held in memory of their mother, and in support of the charities she was involved with, held on June 30, 2007. **BELOW:** On the night of the event, Harry is pictured with American artists Kanye West and P Diddy.

William bends to chat with children after visiting the Valleys Kids project in May 2008. The organisation works with disadvantaged children and their families in the South Wales Valleys region.

BELOW AND OPPOSITE: The courtship, engagement, marriage and subsequent family life of William and his sweetheart Catherine Middleton mirrored that of Charles and Diana some 30 years before. On November 16, 2010, it was announced that William and Kate were to marry – William giving his new fiancée the same ring that belonged to his mother. The wedding took place on April 29, 2011, at Westminster Abbey, with much of the same fanfare and interest – and like Charles and Diana it was not long before the new royal couple started a family. On July 22, 2013, Prince George arrived to become William and Kate's first son and third in line to the British throne. A little less than two years later on May 2, 2015, the couple welcomed a daughter – Charlotte. The royal girl was given the middle name Diana, a touching tribute to the late Princess of Wales.

Prince Harry dons a Christmas hat at Mants'ase Children's Home in Lesotho. During the trip in December 2014, Harry saw first-hand the work done in the time since his previous visits.

BELOW: Prince William, now the Duke of Cambridge, shows that he's at ease with major figures from the world of entertainment. He's pictured, on November 26, 2013, singing with pop sensation Taylor Swift and rock legend Jon Bon Jovi at the Centrepoint charity gala dinner at London's Kensington Palace.
ABOVE: And the following year he's shown on June 4 at a video skills session at the homeless charity's base in Bradford. Diana had been Centrepoint's patron until she died, a position William took over in 2005 – his first patronage.

Diana had enjoyed huge popularity in America, and close ties with its presidents and their spouses during her life. There was huge interest when the Duke and Duchess of Cambridge embarked on a three-day visit to the country in 2014, during which William met President Barack Obama in the iconic Oval Office.

Demonstrating similar commitment and passion for important causes as his mother, Prince Harry has been instrumental in creating and developing the Invictus Games – an international multi-sport event for sick and injured armed services personnel. He's pictured here on May 8, along with key supporter and US first lady Michelle Obama, ahead of the Opening Ceremony of the 2016 games held within the Disney resort at Orlando in Florida.

Mental health was an issue championed by the Princess of Wales, and her work has clearly inspired her sons and the Duchess of Cambridge who joined forces to launch the Heads Together charity which encourages people to come forward and talk about their issues. The organisation was the 2017 London Marathon Charity of the Year, and the royal trio is pictured on April 23, 2017, with runners representing their cause at the event.

Diana - The People's Princess

Image credits

Unless indicated, all photographs used in this publication are courtesy of PA Images.

GROUP CREDITS:

EMPICS Archive
EMPICS Entertainment
EMPICS Sport
PA Archive
PA News
PA Wire
Ronald Reagan
Presidential Library
S&G Barratts
Sunday Times
The Times
White House Photo

INDIVIDUAL CREDITS:

Andrew Parsons
Anthony Devlin
Anwar Hussein
Barry Batchelor
Ben Curtis
Butler
Chris Bacon
Chris Jackson
Daniel Leal-Olivas
Dave Thompson
David Cheskin
David Giles
David Jones
Dominic Lipinski
Duncan Raban

Fiona Hanson
John Giles
John Stillwell
Luke MacGregor
Lynne Cameron
Malcolm Croft
Martin Keene
Michael Stephens
Mike Forster
Mike Maloney
Neil Munns
Oliver Douliery
Owen Humphreys
Paul Rogers
Pete Souza

Rebecca Naden
Robin Nunn
Roger Allen
Ron Bell
Rui Vieira
Sam Pearce
Sean Dempsey
Stefan Rousseau
Stephen Hird
Steve Etherington
Steve Parsons
Toby Melville
Tony Harris

The Royal Collection

Available from classicmagazines.co.uk